OAK LODGE SCHOOL
ROMAN ROAD
DIBDEN PURLIEU
SOUTHAMPTON
SO4 5RO

With best wishes
Mary Rose Baker

CATS' TAILS

Mary Rose Baker

ATHENA PRESS
LONDON

CATS' TAILS
Copyright © Mary Rose Baker 2004

All Rights Reserved

No part of this book may be reproduced in any form
by photocopying or by any electronic or mechanical means,
including information storage or retrieval systems,
without permission in writing from both the copyright
owner and the publisher of this book.

ISBN 1 84401 303 0

First Published 2004 by
ATHENA PRESS
Queen's House, 2 Holly Road
Twickenham, TW1 4EG
United Kingdom

Printed for Athena Press

CATS' TAILS

*To my friend Karen.
Also to my granddaughters Cathy and Debi.*

Chapter I

It was the tenth day in our new home; a warm, sunny morning in July. But where was Christopher? Usually he was waiting, rubbing around our legs, meowing loudly for his breakfast. This day he was missing. There was no answer to our calls. We felt a little anxious but not really worried; if he had wandered off and lost his way in a new district he had our telephone number on the disc around his neck.

Nevertheless, John decided to look around outside and I was relieved soon afterwards to see him walking up the garden path with puss tucked under his arm. Then John saw me at the window and started to shake his head from side to side. I hurried out and there was my lovely Blue Burmese with blood on his little face, quite stiff and cold. He had obviously been knocked by a car and had either managed to reach the grass verge or had been placed there.

Added to our distress was the realisation that we would not be able to keep a cat by this busy road, especially when a neighbour said she too had lost a cat similarly and would not have another.

However, we still had Thomas and Jack, two elderly black-and-white cats, who we had also brought from our previous farm home. They were not frisky or mischievous like our Burmese had been, and they showed no inclination to wander off, but during the next few years each, in turn, died from natural causes and was buried in the garden alongside Christopher.

We now felt quite lonely and lost without a cat in our home.

Then we met Karen, who had set up her own registered charity – 'Bristol's League for Cats'. She showed us the cats she had awaiting homes but agreed we did not live in a suitable place to take one. 'You could always foster,' she suggested. 'We would put a pen in your garden and you could look after one or more until we found them a permanent home.'

This sounded hopeful, but I wasn't keen on the garden idea, especially as it was now late December. 'We have a large garden room, bright and sunny, which our cats used to enjoy,' I said. 'We fitted an electric radiator so they would be warm and cosy in the cold weather.'

Karen agreed this was fine and it was arranged that as soon as she had a suitable cat for us she would let us know.

We were so excited and quickly prepared our room in readiness. It was not long before we heard that one was being brought to us the following Sunday...

Chapter II

Sadie

We were impatient for our first cat to arrive, and finally on Sunday afternoon, as promised, little Sadie was delivered to us, together with her bed, tins of food and bags of litter. Such a poor little scrap, her semi-long fur scruffy and full of flea dirt. My first impression of her, as I took her on my lap, was one of bitter disappointment. Then she raised her head and I found myself looking into a sweet little face with the most beautiful green eyes. I stroked her gently, she purred, and I was completely won over.

After a cuddle she was soon sound asleep, so John and I went through to the kitchen to fill her food and water dishes for when she awoke.

When we returned to the garden room Sadie had completely disappeared! There were only two chairs in the room and a tall, upright freezer in the corner. She wasn't behind that, although we kept looking. The windows were shut and there was no fireplace for an escape up the chimney. We kept calling her name but there was no response.

'She can't be underneath the freezer,' John said, 'but I shall have to pull it out.'

It was heavy but he managed it and then, of course, we saw the opening which housed the condenser. John could feel Sadie's fur and managed with some difficulty to pull her out. She had been stuck in there, getting warmer by the minute and quite unable to back out herself. The only one not in shock was Sadie, who was soon tucking into her tea as if nothing untoward had happened! John had to box in the freezer to avoid a repetition.

Next day I spent a long time brushing and combing her tortoiseshell-and-white fur and playing with her, not that she understood toys or even a ball. She was only a year old and had been very neglected, especially with regard to fleas. She now had a severe flea allergy, and although Karen had treated her before sending her to us she would need a monthly treatment for the rest of her life.

We soon noticed Sadie shaking her head and discovered she had ear mites. John took on the task of cleaning her ears with cotton wool soaked in olive oil. It was amazing the amount of mites and dirt that came out each time. Sadie loved this performance and purred loudly.

I weighed her after a week and she was only four pounds. However, with daily grooming and thanks to an enormous appetite – we only had to mention the word food and she was there – she soon started to put on weight and become a very pretty cat. She even ate the tablets from the vet as if they were sweets, the only cat I've ever known to do this! After five weeks her weight had risen to six pounds, which seemed just right for her size.

In the meantime it was realised that Sadie had not been spayed. Before any cats could be homed by the charity they had to be neutered, so off we went to the vet with her. After a worming treatment too we could concentrate on fun and games.

Her favourite game was football in the hall, which we played most days until I was exhausted. She loved balls. One day John and I had a day in Exmouth and spotted a small red rubber ball in the road. We took it home, washed it well and presented it to Sadie. She was ecstatic and that one became her favourite. A real football instead of the lightweight table tennis-types!

Sadie's other game involved following me upstairs and

then racing me down from the landing. She always gave me a head start and then bounded past me on the last couple of stairs. Then she enjoyed a big hug and lots of praise for being the winner.

Now the weather was improving we decided she needed some fresh air, so we bought a harness and walked her around the garden. Every day was filled with delight for both of us. Although I longed for her to be chosen for a loving home of her own, I now dreaded the thought of losing her.

One day Karen rang, asking us to collect a nine-year-old black female cat named Sydney. We quickly changed that name to Cindy, which seemed more appropriate! Her meeting with Sadie was a disaster. Although Sadie ran forward eagerly to make friends the new cat hissed and growled at her. We allowed them a few days to settle down but there was no improvement, so we were forced to keep them separated as much as possible.

Just three months after Sadie came to us, a very nice couple with two young children arrived to adopt her. They loved her on first sight, but poor little Sadie sensed what was happening and tried to hide. It was heartbreaking to see her frantic struggles when they were putting her into the carrier. I pushed her little red ball in with her, then had to stand back and let her go. I missed her so much in the following days, especially when there was no little puss waiting in the hall to welcome us whenever we came home.

After a few weeks I visited Sadie in her new home in anticipation of a loving reunion, but it wasn't to be. I saw her playing happily with the two young children and looking so well. She didn't turn around, nor did she recognise my voice when I spoke to her new owner. I resisted touching her or speaking to her, but quietly came away content that she was in the loving home she deserved. I was determined not to get so emotionally involved in future!

Chapter III

Cindy

Cindy was homeless due to her owners' broken marriage. She was nine years old, a short-haired black cat who, apart from a flea allergy, also had dermatitis. The vet gave her a steroid injection and I started grooming her, which soon improved her appearance. Her appetite was poor and John spent ages upstairs on the landing, persuading her to eat various treats. She was very friendly and loving with both of us, but the sight of another cat drove her wild. She attacked Sadie on a couple of occasions and her sharp claws drew blood. The other cats we fostered later had the same effect on her.

She enjoyed her walk in the garden on the harness, and was no trouble on her own. She had taken to eating her meals on the landing and sleeping there too. It was carpeted and warm, with a window reaching down almost to floor level which gave her a good view of the garden. John left his bedroom door open at night and she spent most of the time on his bed. It was a double bed but she insisted on sleeping in the middle, edging him to one side, so it was no surprise when he fell out one night!

How we longed for Cindy to be offered a home, but nearly four months passed before Karen rang to say she had somebody interested. It was an elderly lady who she knew quite well so this sounded promising. The next day we took Cindy there and all seemed well. She looked around, walked up and down the stairs and purred loudly, obviously pleased with her new home. We felt very relieved when we left her there.

The other two cats we had at this time were also due to leave us the following evening, so we arranged to go off visiting the following week while we were free.

The very next morning we had a nasty shock when Karen rang to say Cindy was being returned as the lady had decided not to keep her! We explained that we had made arrangements to go away on Monday so couldn't have her back.

On Sunday we had to see Karen with the adoption forms and were upset to learn Cindy was in a cage at the vets until an outdoor pen became available. She couldn't go indoors because of her behaviour towards other cats – in any case there was no room. How unhappy she was going to be after all her freedom. On a sudden impulse I announced that we would adopt her ourselves! John was surprised but agreed, and Karen was relieved. She immediately rang the veterinary practice and arranged for us to collect Cindy there and then, and in no time at all we were home with our very own cat. We had no fear of this one wandering beyond the garden.

Of course there was the problem that we were off to North Devon the following morning, but fortunately our daughter readily agreed to come in twice daily to feed her. So that took care of Cindy, no longer a fostered cat.

Chapter IV
Bella and Maddy

The day after Sadie left us we visited Karen and collected two eighteen-month-old cats. They had been homed four months earlier and the man had just returned them to her complaining that they were unfriendly, hid in corners and bit and scratched. We felt rather apprehensive, but it was a challenge and a different experience for us.

They were named Maddy and Bella. Maddy was a very large tabby and Bella quite small and black and white. It was difficult to realise they were the same age; in fact, one friend assumed they were mother and kitten.

They were extremely nervous when they arrived and Maddy did have a tendency to stay in a corner, but that same evening Bella spent an hour sleeping on my lap. There wasn't much wrong with her!

Maddy was quite different, she kept away from us and I kept away from her. I didn't fancy being scratched and bitten! She was enjoying her food and beginning to move around in their room, so after a couple of days I went in there and sat on a chair. She watched me for a while and then, to my surprise, walked across and sat beside me. Somewhat nervously I stroked her. She enjoyed it and purred, finally rubbing against my legs. Soon she liked being combed and would even lie on her back to have her tummy tickled. It was gratifying to have them both friendly so soon, but they were still rather nervous, especially Maddy where John was concerned. I think a man must have frightened her at some time.

They loved their own room but were reluctant to join us in the rest of the house, although they eventually ventured into the adjoining dining room. Bella liked to jump on the dining chairs, but when I discovered she was scratching the cloth seats we decided to remove them. Next time she jumped up she was very surprised to fall straight through to the floor!

We had read that music was very relaxing for animals, so we decided to try out some CDs on them. It was amusing to see them, stretched out and contented, listening to Strauss waltzes, which appeared to be their favourite. Maddy was improving daily, and to my delight had even taken to playing football.

One day we took Cindy into their room hoping that she would become friendly with these two. It was not a successful meeting. She hissed, displaying a menacing expression, which caused Maddy to do likewise and spring at her. John managed to grab Cindy and remove her before they could harm each other.

After a month we started getting enquiries from people interested in homing Maddy, but no one was prepared to take Bella with her. Finally a lady rang saying she might consider taking two cats and would like to see them. She was single and lived alone in a very nice house, which sounded ideal.

We were so anxious that they behaved themselves, not be nervous or try to hide away. We need not have worried. Julia came into the room, knelt down and called them and Maddy and Bella ran towards her, tails in the air and very friendly. It was love at first sight for all of them! This time their homing was a great success. I still receive regular reports of them from Julia. She even takes them on caravan holidays, which they greatly enjoy!

BELLA AND MADDY

Chapter V

Tansy

No sooner had Maddy and Bella left us than Karen had two more cats waiting for a foster home. One was Sophie, a Birman with a severe digestive problem, and the other was Tansy, a sweet little black-and-white semi-feral cat, with beautiful green eyes.

Tansy had spent her short life living wild in the grounds of a large hotel. At a very young age she had her first litter of kittens but evaded capture. This time Karen, with assistance, had managed to rescue her in time to have her second litter in warmth and comfort.

Once these kittens had found good homes Tansy was ready to come to us. She needed to become accustomed to living in a house before she was found a permanent home, and we were happy to have her. Any wildness in her nature had been tamed by Karen's gentle treatment of her and the kittens. We found her friendly and quite delightful. It took a while to get her used to a litter tray, but we forgave her for early accidents!

The day of her visit to a vet to be spayed and microchipped arrived. She was no trouble and as bright as usual afterwards. The following afternoon we were out visiting a cousin, and when we returned at teatime we put down Tansy's food and started our own meal. I looked in to check that Tansy was eating hers as she had seemed rather reluctant: she had eaten nothing. She stood there looking miserable, with her stomach very bloated. Her litter tray was unused and we realised that neither of us had emptied it since her operation. I panicked!

'She'll have to see the vet. I'll ring and make sure it's surgery time.' I was told we must get her there in twenty minutes, otherwise it would be too late.

Poor John! He left his tea half-eaten, whisked her into the car and set off. He had to travel from Nailsea to Whitchurch in Bristol in twenty minutes, which seemed almost impossible during the busy rush hour. Fortunately the last animal was still being treated when he arrived, so Tansy was in time to be examined.

Meanwhile I waited anxiously at home. At last I heard the car draw up and rushed to open the door. 'Is she all right?' I asked.

'Not yet,' John replied. 'We have to give her an enema! The vet said it would work within ten minutes which would mess up the car, so we have to manage it ourselves.'

This was easier said than done. It was my job to keep Tansy still, but she was having none of it. Finally, in desperation, I grabbed her by the scruff of her neck to immobilise her, held her aloft, and John quickly inserted the enema. Probably not the way a vet would have done it, but it worked. After ten minutes Tansy felt much better and quickly forgave us for the indignity.

Five days later she was due to have her stitches out. The head nurse attended to her and we were pleasantly surprised when she told us that she had homed one of Tansy's kittens.

In June we were having a spell of dry, warm weather so I decided to try Tansy on the harness. She did not like it! She struggled, twisted and turned, lay on her back and would have tried the patience of a saint. But I was no saint. I picked her up and returned her to the house. 'Never to be repeated,' I told John.

Of course I relented and soon she did better, but she was never happy with the harness.

It was getting too warm in the garden room with the sun

shining in all morning. John had the brilliant idea of fitting a frame within the French doors and fixing weld mesh to it. We were then able to open the doors so that fresh air came through. It was a great improvement and the cats were safe to lie there.

One day when Tansy and I were walking down the garden path she spotted Cindy between the rows of potatoes and made a dash for her. She pulled so hard on the lead that I almost fell over. To my amazement Cindy took to her heels and was over the garden fence in a flash. This confirmed our suspicion that it was fear which caused Cindy's aggression towards other cats.

In August we had a visit from a reporter on the local newspaper, interviewing us and taking photographs of us with Tansy and Sophie. Karen had arranged this in the hope of getting more cats homed or finding more fosterers in our area. We were rather disappointed to receive no enquiries after this.

Tansy finally took to playing with a ball, and I often discovered her happily kicking it around on her own. She was a very contented little cat.

We had great pleasure from her for three months until she finally went to a very good home in Clevedon. We shall never forget Tansy.

Chapter VI

Sophie

We fostered Sophie from May to September 1999. She was a beautiful Seal Point Birman with thick, creamy fur, golden patches on her back and startlingly blue eyes. She was the first pedigree cat to come to us.

Unfortunately she was in poor health, suffering from severe digestive problems and on a diet of fish only. This was a problem with other cats around, so we decided to put her in our small bedroom.

She seemed so docile that we were totally unprepared for the excitement when she arrived. Cindy and Tansy had crept up the stairs to investigate, and as John released Sophie from the carrier she spotted them and gave chase. Hissing and yowling, they all dashed down the stairs, around the dining room and back upstairs for quite six times before we were finally able to separate them and restore peace and order!

Sophie ate her fish slowly with little enthusiasm, and she often stayed in her little armchair when it was taken in to her. Sometimes she remained sleeping and had to be lifted down to her dish.

One day when John was using the vacuum cleaner upstairs he took it into her room and was surprised when she ignored the noise. Cats are usually terrified of it. We realised then that she was quite deaf, which also explained why she took no notice when I spoke to her. It also accounted for other strange behaviour.

After three weeks we were tired of cooking fish each day

and Sophie was tired of eating it. She had a very poor appetite and we were getting worried about her. She was due for a check-up with the vet and we discussed her diet with him. We had already tried a little chicken, which she enjoyed, and he suggested rabbit for an alternative. A great idea, except that we were unable to buy a rabbit anywhere. A fishmonger told us he wouldn't be getting any for a couple of months as summer was the wrong time of year for them.

We were determined to find a rabbit so we phoned Fred, a farmer friend in North Devon, and asked him to shoot one for us. He shot two, we collected them, John skinned them, froze one and we cooked a portion of the other for Sophie. After all that fuss she didn't like rabbit and refused to eat it! Luckily, Cindy and Tansy thoroughly enjoyed this unexpected treat.

We next decided to experiment with tins of gourmet and Hill's dried food (meant for kittens). This was a great success. She looked forward to her meals, put on some weight and became much livelier, too lively as it turned out!

One very hot afternoon John noticed what appeared to be a small dog outside our porch door. He opened the front and porch doors and in rushed Sophie. She raced straight up the stairs, two at a time, and waited outside her bedroom door! Because of the heat-wave John had opened the side window just a fraction and she had noticed this, squeezed through and jumped or fallen some twelve feet onto the bricked drive below, amazingly none the worse for this escapade! Next day John made a guard for Sophie's window.

We started taking her into the garden. She didn't need the harness and lead. In fact, the first few times she was soon back at the front door asking to go in. She didn't like the wind ruffling her fur, but on a still day she would walk along the side of the house and finally ventured into the back garden. Here she was a different cat. She ran round and round the lawn and really enjoyed herself, and at these times she looked a normal, healthy cat.

Karen was now able to advertise Sophie as needing a home. Eventually a couple called to see her. They already had a Birman and were interested in Sophie, but next day they rang to say they had decided not to take her, possibly because she was deaf? I felt she should really be an only cat as her diet still had to be followed carefully.

It was a month later, after a further advert, that Jenny came and fell in love with Sophie. She worked in the daytime, but since Sophie loved to sleep for hours on end this would be no problem. We explained about the diet and did a home visit and found everything very satisfactory. Lucky Sophie – she had found a very kind and loving owner, but this wasn't the end! Two weeks later Jenny rang to say Sophie had diarrhoea and was very poorly. Her old trouble had returned. We collected her to take her to the vet and Karen suggested Jenny should choose another cat. Sophie finally went to Jane and Dave, who were also fosterers, and she was very happy with them. We already had two more cats.

Chapter VII

Six Kittens

Shortly before Tansy and Sophie left us, Robin, Karen's husband, presented us with a new and quite different job.

Six kittens had been discovered, hidden in a container ship when it docked in Portsmouth. Their mother was missing and they were urgently needing attention. Kennels in Brent Knoll were willing to accept them, but Karen was asked to send someone occasionally to cuddle and socialise them, as the staff were kept too busy to manage this.

We arranged to go every Friday morning. We were surprised on our first visit at the overall size of the kennels. First we had to pass the dogs in their individual outside runs, all barking and wagging their tails when they spotted us, then into the cats' section; a very long corridor with large indoor pens on one side, each with an outside run.

Finally we reached the two pens allocated to our six kittens, three in each one. It was quite difficult for the kennel maid to let us into a pen without letting the lively kittens out. They were pretty little creatures, three blacks, two tabbies and one tortoiseshell.

Once alone with them we discovered they were little hooligans, their only aim being to run up our legs and backs; a painful experience. There was nowhere for us to sit down and cuddle them, but it would have made no difference. They only wanted fun and games, and although there were balls, toys and a scratch post provided, their only idea of fun was climbing all over us. They appeared to see us as giant scratch posts! What a relief to be let out and ushered in with the other three – only to discover these were even worse! My tights were torn and my legs covered in scratches by the time we left.

Before our next visit we both purchased cheap trousers and wore our oldest tops. This time we went singly into each pen and asked to be let out in twenty minutes. It actually felt like two hours!

We took some lengths of baler cord with us as this had always proved a favourite with our other cats, and this certainly helped. They loved catching the ends, pulling and biting with gusto. It was quite tiring, actually, twirling two cords in one hand and one in the other to keep these hyperactive little devils occupied. Any slacking and the penetrating claws were active again!

We continued these visits for eighteen weeks. I hope the kittens felt better for it, but I can't say that we did! However, we did enjoy driving onto the sands at Brean afterwards, to enjoy a picnic lunch and to wind down.

The kittens had always greeted us enthusiastically and it was rewarding to see them finally grown big and strong, ready to go to caring homes. I must say that they had very good treatment at the kennels.

Chapter VIII

Thomas and Rosie

We were warned that ginger Thomas was a feisty cat and very difficult to handle, so John put on some old leather gauntlets, previously used for prickly hedge trimming, and attempted to remove him from Sue's outdoor pen into a carrier. Thomas went berserk. He fought and hissed and tried to bite. Eventually he did bite, through the glove to John's finger and right through to the bone. (It subsequently turned septic.)

I was terrified of him. We decided that once he was in the cat room we would not attempt to touch him but ignore him completely.

His sister Rosie, also ginger and white, was easier to handle, although not averse to giving me a nip now and again!

Thomas would not use the bed provided or one of the easy chairs but preferred a tattered cardboard box which had been left in a corner of the room. From here he watched our comings and goings. Ignoring him paid off. A few days later I sat on a chair and had eye contact with him and he came forward and rubbed round my legs. He also rubbed round John when he took the food in. Soon I was able to stroke him and finally to comb his thick fur, which was very matted towards his tail end, but only a very little at a time, I must admit, and sometimes when he was busy eating!

Rosie was soon kicking a ball around and Thomas liked to play with a length of baler cord which I dangled in front of him. He could get rid of any aggression by biting at that!

Eventually we left their door open in the evenings. Rosie would rush in first, jump onto my lap and was soon fast asleep. Thomas would stand there watching her, rather jealously, but sometimes jumped onto the settee and rested his head on John's knee.

We thought we had him well tamed until a visit to the vet. During the journey he had a panic attack; a strange sound came from him. His mouth was open and he seemed to have difficulty breathing. This happened three times. A nightmare journey! In the waiting room he was calm and quite recovered. In the treatment room the head nurse stepped forward smiling to get him out of the carrier when he decided to turn feral again. She must have jumped quite two feet in the air when confronted by this ferocious wild animal.

'I'll have to fetch a vet,' she said. Alas! He suffered similarly and decided to take Thomas to another room. Finally they returned, with the vet admitting ruefully that he had been bitten through the blanket he had used to cover Thomas! Once home he was all sweetness again.

Thomas loved his toys, especially a lamb. One evening he brought his mouse in to us, entertained us by tossing it about for a few minutes, and then returned it to his room.

Karen provided us with two hooded loos which prevented the litter from being scratched over the floor. The cats loved them and it was amusing to see them going in and out, except that Thomas tended to set on Rosie as she emerged from hers. It was just teasing on his part, and they really got on very well together.

On firework night we had our own cat, Cindy, in with us. Usually she had to be shut in the kitchen as she was very nervous of other cats, but now all three were together for the first time. Cindy stayed under the chair, hissing and making horrible faces, while Thomas sat on another chair watching her with interest. The following night with the bangs still continuing, the three were together again. It was soon evident that Thomas was falling for Cindy in a big way. He couldn't take his eyes off her and finally took a few tentative steps towards her. This time he was on the receiving end of the feral treatment and quickly backed off. He did try twice more with the same result, so was forced to give up all hopes of a romance. Rosie slept on.

When it was time for them to leave us we were anxious about putting Thomas in a carrier. We popped his mouse and lamb in with him and he immediately started to play with the lamb. He was quite relaxed. What a difference from the cat we had collected three months before!

Chapter IX

Trapping Feral Cats

We now had a rest from fostering for almost a year. Instead we helped in various other ways, mainly in trapping feral cats.

The first call came from Portishead where a few ferals had taken over a private garden. There was a mother cat there with kittens and the owner of the house was anxious for them to be collected and looked after properly. Robin provided us with a trap and a tin of mackerel in tomato sauce!

When we arrived the lady greeted us with good news. She had put down food in a small greenhouse attached to the house and had managed to shut the cat and kittens in there. She assured us there was no way out for them, so this appeared to be an easy job for us.

The greenhouse was packed with rubbish and cardboard boxes and the kittens were hidden away in a corner. John decided to go in alone with the cat carrier – we were relieved the trap wasn't needed, as we had never set one before. He had no trouble popping the kittens in; then turned round to catch their mother. She scrambled up a pile of boxes and disappeared through a hole in the roof! A pane of glass was missing which unfortunately was unseen from below.

We decided to set the trap for the mother cat, who we hoped would come back later. We took the babies to Karen, who was very experienced in dealing with young kittens. As for the trap; the only cat ever caught in that was a tom cat!

We finally had to give up on the mother who had completely disappeared.

Trapping cats from a feral colony was one of the most interesting jobs that John and I undertook. The cats had taken residence in the grounds and outbuildings of a large country hotel where they were well fed in return for keeping down the rats and mice. Unfortunately, their numbers were increasing due to the occasional arrival of kittens, and the only solution was to trap them and get them neutered.

We set our first trap, placing some tasty tinned mackerel inside – something that few cats can resist. The following morning we heard that one had fallen for the bait. We collected her early, took her to the vet in Whitchurch where she was spayed, collected her in the afternoon and returned her to the hotel. How that cat raced off to rejoin her friends! We then returned home to Nailsea feeling well satisfied. It involved a total journey of forty-five miles!

During the next fortnight we caught five females and one tom cat, all equally wild, hissing and growling, but thankfully harmless in the trap. The vet had to handle these!

One day a solitary kitten was caught in the trap, looking so pitiful we couldn't resist it! We no longer had a 'cat' room as our garden room had been redecorated and refurnished. We collected an indoor pen from Karen and once again we were fostering, despite our intention to give up.

A few days later three more kittens were trapped together. By the time we arrived the kitchen staff had already helped themselves to two of them, but found the third one too wild to handle. That meant a second one for us – a very special one as it transpired...

Our job was now finished here as the trap remained empty until we finally removed it.

Chapter X

Two Trapped Kittens

Tabs

This was the first feral kitten we had trapped, a beautiful little tabby, so very frightened, hissing and scared of being touched. We put a protective cover on the dining table, set up an indoor pen and popped her in. She made a beeline for the bed, nestled against a fluffy toy rabbit and sat there staring at us with big eyes. We left her with food and water and when I returned later the food had gone. I whispered a few sweet nothings to her and she just blinked her eyes and settled down to sleep. *She'll be no trouble*, I thought.

Next morning John was first in to see Tabs. The pen was empty! No sign of a cat anywhere. We searched the room and eventually discovered her on a shelf, hiding behind some books and once again very, very scared. It was a mystery as there was no obvious way out with the door still tightly shut. Karen suggested that she had squeezed through above the door where the bars were a little wider apart. Fixing some wide tape over these prevented a further escape.

Once Tabs had recovered from this escapade she soon settled down. Although still nervous and very quiet she allowed us to stroke her and to be lifted onto my lap. Eventually she started to purr, which was so rewarding, but I still felt she was too quiet.

I thought another kitten might enliven her, and just a few days later a second one was caught in the trap, a real feral kitten this time, hissing and yowling, struggling and scratching. Tabs appeared to disapprove of this behaviour but allowed it to share her bed, although she became even quieter and more withdrawn. I took her out of the pen as often as possible, nursing, brushing and combing her, all of which she loved. It was a great relief when Kim and her two children came and decided to give her a home. I'm sure she has been very happy with them.

Katy

At first we called our second feral kitten Tich because it was smaller than Tabs, but otherwise a very similar tabby and it turned out to be another little girl. The similarity ended there, for she was the wildest creature you could imagine. When we approached the pen she would hiss, flatten her ears and get ready to spring at us, her face contorted with fury. How such a small animal could put fear into us I don't know, but she certainly did.

John always opened the cage to put her food in or to change her litter tray and was always met with the same reception. I was too scared to try it! This continued for two weeks, during which time I spent a considerable amount of my day sitting beside the pen talking quietly to her. It worked because she stopped hissing at me.

We still couldn't touch her, so John suggested we bought a baby's brush and tied it to a garden cane. When she was lying with her back to the door it was possible to stroke her gently with the brush, and she actually enjoyed this as long as our hands were nowhere near her. Next I put my hand against the cage and she came forward to sniff it: no hisses. This encouraged me to try stroking her and this she allowed. All this time she still hissed and snarled at John.

She had a ping-pong ball in her pen which she started to play with, so I decided to join in and we were soon having a fine game. I would roll the ball towards her and she, leaning over the side of her bed, would tap it back. Then I tried throwing the ball in and she would catch it in her two paws!

After four weeks with us, when we were playing and I stroked her she started purring. It went on for about five minutes and I knew that we had bonded at last. I was so happy that I hugged her and she purred again. At this point I decided to call her Katy.

I still had to persuade her to walk out of the pen on her own. She just liked to be lifted out and nursed. John had started to go in on his own each evening to play ball with her, but she still hissed each time although she enjoyed the game. Almost eight weeks went by before she purred for John, yet still she couldn't resist a gentle hiss at him, just force of habit.

Soon we removed the pen, but she still liked her bed on the table. She would jump up and down and race around the floor after her ball, then stop for a cuddle. Such a special little cat, and one of the most loving I have ever fostered.

Karen found Katy a lovely home with a very kind couple, and I have since received a photograph of her at one year old, looking very, very beautiful. I only wish she were mine!

KATY

Chapter XI
The Black-and-White Boys

Karen had three young black-and-white cats brought to her, all needing new homes. They were brothers and all extremely nervous and proved difficult to manage together. She decided to split them up by sending them to us one at a time. Their names were Archie, Alex and Arnie.

Archie was the first to come, brought one evening by Karen and Robin. He was certainly nervous of everything, including us. He ignored the food we put down, so we left him alone for the night. His dish was empty next morning and he was settled very comfortably in his bed. He didn't seem too pleased to see us though, and his big black eyes showed his nervousness. I popped into the room a couple of times that morning, which caused him to run under a chair or hide behind the curtain. I didn't attempt to touch him, just spoke gently and left him alone again.

In the afternoon I spent an hour with him and soon he was rubbing around my legs, purring loudly, and his eyes were back to normal. John tried later on and when he sat down Archie jumped up on him and purred. Unfortunately he did not touch his food that day. In the evening we tried a different variety: still no interest. We left both kinds down, together with some dry food. Next morning it was *all* gone!

Archie was becoming very friendly with us both, but was still nervous of noise in the kitchen or hall. Then he discovered the windowsill by the radiator and became very relaxed lying there and even the noises failed to worry him.

He did jump down quickly when John went past with

the roller one afternoon. By the time John returned with it Archie was on his back legs watching through the window with keen interest. With his white front and standing upright he reminded me of a little penguin.

A few days later I phoned Karen to say that he was ready for a new home. I didn't want him to become too attached to us. Unfortunately there were no requests for a cat at this time, so it was arranged that Archie would go back with one of his brothers while Alex would come to us.

We took him back one Sunday morning and exchanged him with Alex, who apart from slightly different facial features, was a look-alike, not nearly as nervous however. Apart from the actual journey and coming into a strange house, he soon settled down and was quite laid back. He ate well and quickly discovered the windowsill.

That very same evening Karen rang to say Frances in Clevedon had rung, wanting an 'unassuming' cat. She was prepared to wait for a few days. I wanted Archie to go to her, but I had to get Alex ready as a 'special' cat was to be brought to us at the end of the week. It was all very mysterious. I had never encountered an 'unassuming' cat, and I wasn't sure about the 'special' cat. Fortunately, Alex was behaving very well. He didn't need our company as much as Archie had done, but he was very friendly.

On Wednesday I did a home-check and found Frances, and her home, very suitable. She came to meet Alex the following day, liked him and arranged to collect him on Friday afternoon. He was particularly friendly that morning, on my lap for ages and wanting to kiss me!

Frances was most excited when she came to collect him and they went off quite happily together.

Some days later I was delighted to receive a card from her – a picture of a black-and-white cat – with a reassuring message inside. She wrote:

Just a short note to let you know how Alex is settling in to his new home. He is a very affectionate little cat and loves to be made a fuss of. He is still a little jumpy but has a prime spot on top of the wardrobe in our spare bedroom, where he spent his first three days. He can watch the world go by and sits and purrs to himself. He has become quite playful and is chasing a ball around my feet as I write this. He is also slowly stripping my spider plants of all their runners! He is getting on quite well with my other cat – they seem to have agreed to ignore each other!

Best wishes, Frances

In the meantime I heard from Karen that Archie and Arnie were doing well and they eventually found a home together.

Chapter XII

Gracie

Gracie was the 'special' cat we were expecting. She was certainly different – a pedigree Cornish Rex. It is difficult to describe her. She was definitely strange looking: rather thin, possibly because of her smooth and velvety crimped coat. It wasn't fur in the manner of other domestic cats and was strange to the touch. I wasn't very impressed by her appearance and would have preferred the third black-and-white cat, but Gracie needed special attention. She had been used for breeding but we heard she had not been a good mother, so she was now spayed and looking for a new home.

The first night with us Gracie was kept in a pen on the table. The mess she made was unbelievable! She scattered litter all over the pen, in her bed, her food and even through the bars onto the table and floor. We removed the pen and she immediately jumped around on all the furniture. She was the most vocal cat we had ever known, with a constant, piercing meow.

Her behaviour was entertaining if nothing else. When a young lady approached Karen for a cat she was advised to phone me about Gracie. She wanted to know if the cat jumped, was noisy or scratched! All of these, actually, but I didn't tell her, just suggested she came to see her. She couldn't come until the weekend and I hoped that Gracie would have calmed down by then. She did improve slightly, but kept up a constant conversation. She couldn't help scratching as her claws were so long and sharp. It wasn't intentional. Later on we took her to our own vet to have them cut.

Lucinda arrived on Sunday accompanied by her mother, who had journeyed from Surrey to help her choose a cat. She took one look at Gracie and said that she wanted a white cat! However, she sat on the floor and Gracie immediately snuggled inside her open coat and purred. Her behaviour was faultless and the mother was most impressed. Even Lucinda hesitated, which gave me hope. Then she stood up. 'I'm sorry,' she said, 'I've always set my heart on a white cat,' and off they went.

Four other people came to see Gracie over the next few weeks. Each time she was friendly and behaved impeccably, but nobody wanted her. One lady was very apologetic but said, 'It's no good. I can't take to her. I'd rather have an ordinary moggie.'

She was quite loving with us now and enjoyed being on a lap to wash herself and fall asleep. Neighbours called in to see her out of curiosity and liked her, but none wanted a cat. I began to give up hope of her ever finding a home.

Then one day we had a nasty shock. John had been in the room playing with her and when I went in later there was no sign of Gracie. I noticed the small transom window was open. We always opened this when we were with her and closed it before we came out, but this time John had forgotten. He was busy in the garden and had not seen her there so we both started a hunt, feeling very worried. She had never been out before and was certainly not in our garden or the neighbouring ones. The road was busy with traffic. There was no answer to our calls and I became really frightened. How could I confess to Karen that we had lost the 'special' cat?

After a considerable time I walked sadly back into the house. I could hardly bring myself to open the dining room door, but what joy when I did! There was Gracie bounding towards me, as excited as I was. While I hugged her over and over again she was busy telling me all about her adventure. She just couldn't stop talking! Despite all the excitement I did remember to shut the window before going out to tell John the good news.

When John came in he immediately noticed the muddy paw marks leading up the window to the opening, which showed how she had come back in. We were both delighted with our clever girl. Being an indoor cat and unused to the outdoors it showed intelligence to go walkabout and still find her way back in.

We both became more fond of Gracie after this, which was just as well as she was with us for nine weeks. We let her have a run around the house when Cindy was asleep in the greenhouse. We tried her with the harness and lead for walks in the garden, although she didn't enjoy this. She wanted our company at all times and cried when we left her alone. I couldn't imagine we would ever find the right person to home her. She needed a lonely person who could spend plenty of time with her and who would be rewarded by Gracie's entertaining and loving nature.

Then the miracle happened! We heard of a lady, living alone, who was wanting just such a cat for company. Gracie was taken to her – on approval – and we were told it was a match made in heaven!

Gracie was indeed a 'special' cat.

Chapter XIII

Kitty

Kitty was the next cat to come to us, in exchange for Gracie. I had first known Kitty nearly two years before. Amy, an elderly friend, rang me one day, very tearful because she had just lost a well-loved cat. She asked if I could find her one to replace it. Her requirements were very specific: a young cat, female and preferably tortoiseshell and white.

I discovered that one of our members was fostering just such a cat, all ready to go to a new home. In no time I was delivering her to Amy, who loved her on sight and decided to call her Kitty.

We did not live near her but John and I visited occasionally and saw Kitty growing into a beautiful and contented cat. Amy and her husband, Eddie, treated her like their child and she was fortunate to have found such a caring home. There was a large, ancient apple tree in their garden which she loved to climb.

All seemed perfect until the day I received a frantic call from Amy to say that Kitty had been taken away from her. It appeared that she had gone to the vet who, after giving her a scan, had announced that she was four months pregnant! Amy was very distressed, having been assured by me that Kitty was spayed. She told the vet she couldn't cope with kittens so Kitty had been taken to someone who would look after her until her kittens were weaned. This meant being without Kitty for some weeks.

Later that day we heard from Karen that the next cat coming to us was pregnant. It transpired that it was indeed

Kitty. When I told Amy she was so relieved – her greatest worry had been wondering where her cat would go.

As soon as Kitty arrived and was let out of her pen she came straight towards us, rubbing round and purring. Then she sat in her bed and washed herself, looking thoroughly happy. Her fur was so thick and shiny and she looked the picture of health. As with most of our cats she refused to eat for the first couple of days, although we purposely provided her with her favourites. Finally we put down some tinned salmon which she gobbled up straight away. That did the trick as thereafter she ate whatever we put out for her.

We had been told that she wasn't a lap cat, but when she came into the sitting room with us she liked to sit on the arm of my chair. Eventually she decided to drop onto my lap and this became her favourite place. When it was sunny she favoured the windowsill where she could watch the traffic going by.

As the days passed we started to prepare for the birth of the kittens. As we had no previous experience we were not looking forward to this at all. We kept looking at Kitty and could see no change in her. I told Karen that I didn't think she was pregnant after all, but she said again that the vet had scanned her and must have seen the kittens.

We continued our preparations. We placed the pen on a table in a corner of the dining room and bought a larger bed to accommodate Kitty and her babies. I made a lined covering to fit the back and sides of the pen to make it cosy and draught-proof. I added a soft material to the base. Kitty was most interested in all this and showed her appreciation by jumping up and using the bed frequently. The only things missing were the kittens! Time was up now and Amy was ringing anxiously to ask if they'd arrived. There was still no sign.

A few days later we took her along the road to our own vet, who confirmed our suspicions that she was definitely *not* pregnant and appeared to be extremely well. I felt so sorry for Amy who had been deprived of Kitty for so long, but she was delighted when we returned her later that day. Unfortunately, Kitty kept coming to me so we had to make a quick getaway! However, she soon settled down in her own home after her 'holiday'!

We returned the pen to Karen and said we didn't want another cat. This was just as well as exactly one week later John was rushed into Weston hospital with a strangulated hernia, and cats were now out of the question…

Chapter XIV
Pippa

It was several weeks before we were able to help Karen again. Fostering was now out of the question, but we found other ways to be useful, mainly home-checking. It was always necessary before placing a cat to find that the home was suitable: not on a very busy road and preferably with a safe, enclosed garden with access from a catflap. We explained that they should be kept in for the first two weeks to settle with their new owners. If people wanted a young kitten someone should be at home for at least part of the day. We enjoyed meeting these people, who were obviously cat lovers like ourselves.

Another job we undertook was collecting or delivering cats. One day we picked up a heavily pregnant cat from Worle to take her to Warmley. I kept turning round to check on her as the birth appeared to be imminent, but we made it in time!

A few weeks later Karen rang to say that a feral cat and three kittens had been sighted in Nailsea. A trap had been set and the mother cat was caught in it. Could we please get it into a carrier and re-set the trap? This was easier said than done as this cat was even wilder than other ferals we had encountered. However, wearing thick gloves, John was able to grab her at last and we took her home.

A little later that day we were informed that one of the kittens had been trapped. John borrowed a carrier from our daughter and off he went again. This little kitten led him a dance! Fortunately they were shut in the garage, so when it escaped from John's clutches it could only rush round and round and up the walls, until he finally caught it. We were relieved when mother and kitten were collected from us in the evening and taken to Karen.

The remaining two kittens were caught in the trap overnight. This time our grandson was available to carry them to our house in the trap. As before they were collected later by Karen. They were pretty little creatures, ginger and ginger and white. Yesterday's kitten had been tabby and white, similar to Katy.

All three kittens were in good condition as a kind lady had, despite difficulties, been putting out food for the mother for some time. She owned two dogs who were not cat friendly!

It was unfortunate for Karen that she received a second family of ferals around the same time. After a short discussion with John I volunteered to help her by fostering the little tabby kitten, so she was returned to us in a pen and we called her Pippa.

We were warned she was very feisty so were surprised when, after a couple of hisses, she settled down quietly. It was the same the next day, although she was very nervous and would only eat her food during the night. She didn't want our hands in the pen and when I tried the baby brush on the cane she went berserk and jumped around hissing and yowling. She wasn't interested in playing ball either. If I sat beside her, speaking gently, she promptly fell asleep, which I found rather frustrating!

When we eventually opened the door of her pen she quickly jumped down to the floor and enjoyed running around, but was back up in a flash when she saw her tea being brought in. She started playing around with the ping-pong ball but hissed and growled if I touched it. One evening I was allowed to join in. She seemed so friendly that I took courage and gently stroked her back. It was no good. She hissed and jumped away so quickly that she caused me to jump as well!

For five days after this Pippa stayed in her bed and ignored me, always pretending to be asleep. On the sixth day she decided to play with me again – a new game of hide-and-seek. She would hide in her little tent or behind the curtains, then run back to me and sniff my fingers. I didn't attempt to touch her.

On her twenty-sixth day with us she was back in her pen, playing ball with me again, when she finally allowed me to stroke her. I knew she enjoyed it because she purred for the first time, a loud purr which went on and on. We had bonded at last!

Now I was making great progress with Pippa. I was able to lift her onto my lap, which she really enjoyed. She would touch my face gently with her paw. Once, when I put her back on the table, she jumped straight onto me again, determined to stay there. John was also able to stroke her now. She was ready to be homed.

A few days later, ten-year-old Georgina came with her mother to see Pippa. They played happily together under the table so Pippa passed the test. As soon as their older kitten, Squeak, had been neutered we took Pippa to her new home. Georgie rang us that evening to report that Pippa was purring and liked being nursed. Later on we received a lovely photo of Pippa being washed by Squeak, the two of them cuddled together on Georgie's bed. Such a happy ending.

This was definitely the last cat we could foster as John needed three more operations during the next two years. Fostering had certainly been a wonderful and enjoyable experience for us.

★

Since writing this our own dear Cindy has been put to sleep. It has been a painful loss and we feel very lonely without her. At our age we shall not have another cat. At least we have happy memories of all of them, which will have to suffice.

PIPPA